Verlene,

Thank you f[or]
being a part of our
study small group. I loo[k]
forward to growing in Christ
together in 2006.
Merry Christmas—!
love!
Jill

The Inner Beauty Series ❀
Defining Your Worth in the Eyes of God

DISCOVER *Your* INNER BEAUTY

Charisma
HOUSE
Books about Spirit-Led Living

Lisa Bevere

DISCOVER YOUR INNER BEAUTY by Lisa Bevere
Published by Charisma House
A part of Strang Communications Company
600 Rinehart Road
Lake Mary, Florida 32746
www.charismahouse.com

Unless otherwise noted, all Scripture quotations are from the
Holy Bible, New International Version. Copyright © 1973,
1978, 1984, International Bible Society. Used by permission.

Scripture quotations marked AMP are from the Amplified
Bible. Old Testament copyright © 1965, 1987 by the
Zondervan Corporation. The Amplified New Testament
copyright © 1954, 1958, 1987 by the Lockman Foundation.
Used by permission.

Scripture quotations marked NKJV are from the New King
James Version of the Bible. Copyright © 1979, 1980, 1982
by Thomas Nelson, Inc., publishers. Used by permission.

Cover design by Rachel Campbell

Library of Congress Catalog Card Number: 2001099922
International Standard Book Number: 0-88419-842-1

02 03 04 05   8765432
Printed in the United States of America

Contents

Introduction

t's time to take off the veil that is hindering your inner beauty from shining forth! This fourth booklet in the Inner Beauty series will help you learn to do just that. One way to do that is by learning to show forth the attributes of a woman of God. Second Peter 1:5–9 gives an outline for the healthy development of Christian attributes. First you add goodness to your measure of faith. This includes believing that God is a *good God*. Next you add knowledge to this revelation of goodness, and to knowledge, you add self-control. To this, you add perseverance; to perseverance, you add godliness; to godliness, you add brotherly kindness; and lastly, to brotherly kindness, you add love.

We are promised that if we "possess these qualities in increasing measure, they will keep you from being ineffective and unproductive in your knowledge of our Lord Jesus Christ" (2 Pet. 1:8). These are all measures that can be increased by use and the exercise of our faith.

While we are developing the qualities that are possessed by women of God, we must also get rid of the veil of our past, which hides our inner beauty. We are warned, "If anyone does not have them, he is nearsighted and blind, and has forgotten that he has been cleansed from his past sins" (v. 9).

Nearsighted and blind people have a hard time seeing things accurately. I know; I'm nearsighted. Without the help of my glasses, I do not recognize the form of my own husband until he is within twenty feet of me.

Impaired eyesight causes us to lose our edge and insight. The nearsighted only notice the obvious. Often the obvious overshadows the eternal.

This shortsighted condition makes us forgetful. "Where did I leave my keys?" If the item is not right in front of us, we quickly forget it. Peter said this condition will cause us to forget we have been cleansed. When this knowledge is lost, we will begin to make excuses.

Why would anyone go to the trouble to explain

away something for which they were no longer accountable? If they remembered they have been cleansed, they would simply say, "Oh, that was *before I was made new.*"

While we are developing the qualities that are possessed by women of God, we must also get rid of the veil of our past, which hides our inner beauty.

When we do not obey the truth that has been clearly revealed, we will deceive ourselves. (See James 1.) Our hearts again condemn us if we attempt to make justification for our sins by the works of the flesh and psychology of man. Let's go back to the purpose of salvation. Was it not to restore us to God through the remission of sins and the removal of our past?

When I stand before God, I will stand alone, as

an individual. Each of us is judged for what we have done. That is why I needed a Savior. I had lived a life that could not stand the scrutiny and presence of a holy God. I became a Christian when I experienced this revelation: I was sinful and God was holy. The two could never touch. Jesus became my Mediator.

Job described his need for a Savior this way:

> If only there were someone to arbitrate between us, to lay his hand upon us both.
> —Job 9:33

Don't Look Back!

Looking back makes us unfit for kingdom service. We must again place our hands firmly on the plow and push forward. If we look back while we plow, our rows will be uneven and we will risk breaking our plow blades on rocks or stumps. Plowing requires a constant eye fixed on what is immediately ahead in the field.

The past is gone. It is dead. We need to stop seeking the living among the dead. When we allow our focus to be diverted backward, we forget that we have been cleansed and start to make excuses.

When we look at ourselves in the mirror, we

remember what manner of woman *we had been* and forget what manner of woman *we now are.*

Looking back makes us unfit for kingdom service.

Now it is time to change our focus. It is time to let go of what is gone and to discover that which is hidden within—our inner beauty. *You are not what you have done. You are not what has been done to you. You have been translated from that dark domain onto God's path of light.* Your worth is not found in *what you have done.* It is represented by *what Jesus did for you.* If you really believe what He did was enough to wash away your sins, then you must acknowledge that it was enough to wipe out your past. There are no special cases. No longer are you a woman with a past...you are a woman with a future. A woman who possesses true inner beauty.

Are you ready to let that inner beauty shine forth?

Adapted from Lisa Bevere, *The True Measure of a Woman,* 73–74, 81–82.

INNER BEAUTY TIP

GOD IS

MORE CONCERNED

WITH OUR CONDITION

THAN OUR

COMFORT.

1

Solomon's Search

I know that whatever God does, it shall be
forever. Nothing can be added to it, and
nothing taken from it. God does it, that
men should fear before Him.

—ECCLESIASTES 3:14, NKJV

ur world today has its own measuring stick
for beauty. The goal for many young women
is "becoming one of the world's beautiful
people"—meaning accumulating all the *things* the
world says are necessary to reach the status of
"beauty."

By the world's standard, Solomon would have
belonged to the elite fellowship of beautiful people.
But he learned that the *possession of beautiful things*
is not synonymous with *possessing inner beauty.*

In this chapter we will trace the path of Solomon's search for beauty. As a young child he was tutored in the ways and wisdom of the Lord by his mother, Bathsheba. He was her closest and most treasured son. David had promised her that Solomon would sit upon the throne and succeed him (1 Kings 1:30). The Lord had loved Solomon from the moment of his birth and sent confirmation of Solomon's destiny by the mouth of the prophet Nathan (2 Sam. 12:24–25).

In the light of this, Bathsheba raised Solomon from infancy to be set apart as a prince and ruler over God's people. She instructed him daily in the statues and fear of the Lord. Solomon confirms this repeatedly in Proverbs:

> When I was a boy in my father's house, still tender, and an only child of my mother, he taught me and said, "Lay hold of my words with all your heart; keep my commands and you will live…My son, keep your father's commands and do not forsake your mother's teaching."
>
> —PROVERBS 4:3–4; 6:20

Solomon's father gave him commandments, and his mother taught him. David would speak God's laws or principles, then Bathsheba would explain to the young Solomon how they were to be applied to life. Her words bore insight into relationships, gave warning and instruction and imparted an even deeper desire within Solomon for wisdom.

When Solomon became king he was still a young man. In his exploration of all that was under the sun, he began with the pursuit of pleasure. In his own words:

> I thought in my heart, "Come now, I will test you with pleasure to find out what is good."...I tried cheering myself with wine, and embracing folly—my mind still guiding me with wisdom. I wanted to see what was worthwhile for men to do under heaven during the few days of their lives.
> —ECCLESIASTES 2:1, 3

HAVE WE MISSED ANYTHING?

Doesn't that sound like a lot of us? We were raised by parents who instructed us the best they knew how, teaching us right from wrong in the hope that we would learn from their mistakes. But most of us, as soon as we were on our own, pursued pleasure. We just had to find out what we were missing.

After all, we were eighteen and free to vote and make our own decisions! It was now legal for many of us to drink, and we wanted to cheer ourselves with wine and embrace folly. Sin *does* have pleasure for a season…a short one. It wasn't long before we decided we wanted more out of life. We wanted to make a difference, raise a family, achieve professional and personal goals. So as Solomon did, we moved on to the pursuit of achievement.

> I undertook great projects: I built houses for myself and planted vineyards. I made gardens and parks and planted all kinds of fruit trees in them. I made reservoirs to water groves of flourishing trees. I bought male and female slaves and had other slaves who were born in my house. I also owned more herds and flocks than anyone in Jerusalem before me. I amassed silver and gold for myself, and the treasure of kings and provinces. I acquired men and women singers, and a harem as well—the delights

4

of the heart of man. I became greater by far than anyone in Jerusalem before me. In all this my wisdom stayed with me.

—Ecclesiastes 2:4–9

Initially Solomon was overjoyed by his success. He enjoyed completing projects and living in his many houses. He feasted on the fruit he had cultivated and shared beautiful parks with his subjects. There was an ever-increasing army of male and female slaves who lived to fulfill his every desire. His herds of livestock outnumbered everyone else's. He gathered for himself a treasury of gold, silver, riches and lands. He surrounded himself with the best of the world's culture in the form of art and music. He enjoyed the unlimited sensual pleasure of a harem. He was greater than anyone before him. In all this, wisdom remained his constant companion.

I denied myself nothing my eyes desired; I refused my heart no pleasure. My heart took delight in all my work, and this was the reward for all my labor.

—Ecclesiastes 2:10

He denied himself nothing! His heart delighted

in his work. This delight was in itself a reward for his labor. He loved being king, he loved his work and he loved all that surrounded him! It brought him fulfillment—for a season. Soon *having* the most, *doing* the most and *being* the most were not enough for Solomon.

> Yet when I surveyed all that my hands had done and what I had toiled to achieve, everything was meaningless, a chasing after the wind; nothing was gained under the sun.
> —ECCLESIASTES 2:11

LIKE CHASING THE WIND

What did he mean, *nothing was gained?* Solomon was *the best*. With wisdom's guidance, Solomon looked closer and decided all his achievements were as meaningless as chasing the wind. Think about it! The achievements of the greatest and wisest king were comparable to chasing after something one could never capture.

The winds of time had blown by Solomon and reminded him that he was but a mortal and would someday die. In contrast, the wind would continue to encircle the earth, blowing and dispersing the dust of man's achievements from one generation to the next.

This revelation caused Solomon to despise what he had once loved.

> I hated all the things I had toiled for under the sun, because I must leave them to the one who comes after me. And who knows whether he will be a wise man or a fool? Yet he will have control over all the work into which I have poured my effort and skill under the sun. This too is meaningless. So my heart began to despair over all my toilsome labor under the sun. For a man may do his work with wisdom, knowledge and skill, and then he must leave all he owns to someone who has not worked for it. This too is meaningless and a great misfortune.
> —ECCLESIASTES 2:18–21

The wealth, riches and lands he had joyfully toiled to accumulate had now become a source of vexation to this great king. What he had worked for would eventually be lost. All he had tenderly and diligently cultivated could be squandered in the hands of a foolish king. He realized he could not hold on; he must pass it on. All he had accomplished by years of labor would endure but a moment after he was gone. In contrast, Solomon noted:

> I know that whatever God does, it shall be forever. Nothing can be added to it, and nothing taken from it. God does it, that men should fear before Him.
>
> —ECCLESIASTES 3:14, NKJV

Soon *having* the most, *doing* the most and *being* the most were not enough for Solomon.

Although Solomon was the greatest king who had ever lived or ever would live, what he had built would not endure. He saw that it would all be swept away. He realized that even as the greatest and wisest king, he could only hold it but a moment. No man could ever hold on to it. Yet the stars and heavens shining above the works of Solomon remained steadfast. The sun, moon and stars that lit his kingdom would continue to shine long after Solomon's descendants rested in their graves.

Why would God allow this great frustration in a king He loved? Why did He let Solomon enjoy all he had acquired, only to expose the futility of it? Solomon gave the answer: *God does it, that men should fear before Him.*

It was humbling for Solomon to find out that all his wisdom could not preserve his possessions or lengthen his days. All his glory was like the grass—one day splendid, green and life giving and the next, cut down and swept away. The Book of Ecclesiastes is his lament of this earthly, temporary life. He had glimpsed God's everlasting glory and wisdom and found his own glory waning.

At the end of his life, Solomon concluded:

> "Meaningless! Meaningless!" says the Teacher. "Everything is meaningless!"
> —Ecclesiastes 12:8

How many times have you ended up disillusioned and disappointed by something that once brought you happiness? Like Solomon, each of us, at one time or another, has thought, *If only I achieved this or had that, I would be happy!* However, once we achieve these things we discover that we still are not satisfied. Then we become discouraged, because we thought these things would bring us happiness, not disappointment. We have lost the boost of momentum that comes when one pursues a dream.

Ask yourself the following questions, and record your answers in your journal:

1. Over the course of your life, what did you pursue, thinking it would bring fulfillment, but instead left you disappointed?
2. What goals are you pursuing now?
3. Will you be happy once you achieve them?

THE RIGHT PERSPECTIVE ON "THINGS"

It is important to note that there is nothing wrong with having goals and dreams. God made us with the creative capacity to dream. It is equally important to note that outside of the provision of God, none of us is able to enjoy the blessings He gives us.

> Moreover, when God gives any man wealth
> and possessions, and enables him to enjoy
> them, to accept his lot and be happy in his
> work—this is a gift of God.
>
> —ECCLESIASTES 5:19

God gives wealth, possessions and contentment. Outside of His provision we may have "things" but not peace. This means we cannot enjoy them. Often those with the greatest possessions are tormented with the most worry. They cannot rest and enjoy what they have because they are consumed with thinking of ways to safeguard and expand their riches. Then there is another torment that plagues them. Though they have much, they notice there are those who have even more. They strive, trying to gain as much as their neighbor, and so are never satisfied with what they have in their hands. They lose what they possess, either by holding it too tightly or by grasping for more.

This is a telltale sign of those who have measured themselves by what they have. Possessions are a deceptive measure of worth. There is no lasting stability, because a person's worth is not dependent on the increase or decrease of possessions.

This mentality breeds only fear and insecurity. It would mean a person's worth and value would be assigned to something that is inevitably out of his or her control. There are also theft and calamity to consider, not to mention the warnings contained in Proverbs:

> Cast but a glance at riches, and they are gone, for they will surely sprout wings and fly off to the sky like an eagle.
> —PROVERBS 23:5

This illustrates just how fleeting and elusive riches can be—sprouting wings and flying off like an eagle. Eagles are hard to catch once they have taken flight.

Proverbs 11:28 tells us, "Whoever trusts in his riches will fall, but the righteous will thrive like a green leaf." Riches cannot be trusted; they are here today and gone tomorrow. Riches in and of themselves are not wrong; it is the trusting in them that is wrong. The righteous trust in God, not in riches, and therefore thrive. Thriving means more than just existing. To *thrive* means "to prosper, flourish, succeed, advance, increase, bloom and blossom!"

Possessions are a deceptive measure of worth.

All man could ever want is found in God's righteousness. This is not just a temporary state, because Proverbs 8:18 promises, "With me are riches and honor, enduring wealth and prosperity." With God the blessings endure because they are His. With Him we have a temporary and eternal reward of joy and contentment. It is independent of what we have or do not have, own or do not own.

> Then he said to them, "Watch out! Be on your guard against all kinds of greed; a man's life does not consist in the abundance of his possessions."
>
> —LUKE 12:15

It is an urgent warning that not only do we have to look out for but also guard against measuring ourselves by what we have. It is so subtle that it can creep in without our awareness. It is preached by almost every television commercial.

Its lie is propagated by sitcoms, movies and magazines. The world promises that riches will give you everything you want, make you beautiful, fill your house with the best of everything, surround you with friends, give you influence and power and secure the future for you and your loved ones. But it is a lie.

Our lives are of a much greater worth than *things;* therefore, our lives cannot be measured by things. If our worth were equal to a whole world of things, then God would not have ransomed us with the life of His only Son. Instead, He would have ransomed us with the boundless riches of heaven, where the riches are so immense that gold paves the streets. In God's eyes, our worth is far more precious than gold.

BALANCING THE BLESSINGS

> And I saw that all labor and all achievement
> spring from man's envy of his neighbor. This
> too is meaningless, a chasing after the wind.
> —ECCLESIASTES 4:4

Why are these pursuits comparable to chasing the wind? Because even if I do get whatever I desire, I will soon see something else that I want. I'll be forever reaching, never fulfilled.

After we moved from Dallas, John and I returned to minister at a different church. We were staying in the home of some dear friends and had stopped by a very exclusive department store to get them a "thank you" gift. When we walked in, there was an elaborate display of men's ties that caught John's eye. There were two ties that he was particularly fond of, and he couldn't decide between the two. After a few minutes of deliberation, John had an idea. He would buy one tie, and I would get him the other for Christmas.

At first I wasn't too keen on this; I liked picking out presents for people so I could share in their surprise. I told him I'd think about it. However, I could see that he really wanted that tie. John purchased the one tie while I ran upstairs to see a friend of ours who worked in another department of the store. I returned to the tie counter and bought the other tie. As the salesman carefully wrapped it for me, I started feeling grieved. I thought, *What's going on? This is my spending money, and I'm buying a present for my husband.*

Do I have to pray about every purchase? I took the bag from the salesman and started up the escalator. Halfway up, I felt deeply grieved. I saw John waiting at the top of the escalator.

"What's wrong?" he asked.

"John, I bought you the tie, but I am grieved over it."

"I am grieved as well. I think you should return it."

We went down together and returned the tie. I'm sure the poor salesman thought we were nuts. As I placed the money back in my purse, I heard the Holy Spirit say to me, "The blessings I give you will come with no sorrow. The ones you take for yourself will cause you sorrow."

I made note of the lesson, still wondering why buying a tie for my husband was such a big deal.

A few weeks later we both found out why. John was in Chicago preaching. After the service a man asked John to come by his men's clothing store. The following day, the pastor took John by the store, and the man blessed John with twelve ties, several shirts and a gorgeous winter coat! I believe that if we had purchased the tie for ourselves in

Dallas, God would not have moved upon this man's heart to give to John in such a generous way. We would have grabbed our *one* tie when God wanted to give us *twelve* ties.

OBEDIENCE, NOT FORMULA

This does not mean that every time God has told me not to get something I received the same item in large quantities at a later date. It is not a *formula* that God blesses—it is *obedience.* He is more concerned with our *condition* than our *comfort.* He knows He can bless obedience, because the obedient know that fulfillment is not found in the blessings but in obedience to the One who blesses. This is why Paul said:

> But godliness with contentment is great gain.
> —1 TIMOTHY 6:6

True and great riches are found in godliness with contentment. In living a life of godliness with contentment you will discover your true inner beauty. Too often I have picked up a magazine or catalog featuring the latest trends in home decorating and, overwhelmed by the urge, thought, *I must redecorate in this color scheme!* Then reason would grab me as I realized I was perfectly content with what I had—*until I saw something else.* I decided to fast—stop reading these magazines for awhile. In place of decorating magazines I put out my Bible.

"The blessings I give you will come with no sorrow. The ones you take for yourself will cause you sorrow."

Whenever I read my Bible I felt stronger and refreshed, not discontented. It was amazing how much of my thought life had been dominated by the attractive contents of these magazines. When I did pick them up again, the magazines had no hold on me. They were in the right perspective. I could enjoy their ideas without a sense of frustration.

Like me, you may be surrounded by forces that arouse a desire for more in your life. It may be the lifestyle of the rich and famous. (Why is it that we never see the heartbreak behind the facade?) You may think that if only you could live that lifestyle you would truly be one of the world's beautiful people. Only you know your heart and the passions that may drive it.

One truth is certain—*you are not what you own.* Nor will what you own enable your inner beauty to shine forth. In reality, possessions may hinder your inner beauty from being seen.

As you continue reading, I pray that God will help you to grasp His divine secret to true beauty—beauty comes from who you are, not from what you own.

Adapted from *The True Measure of a Woman*, 39–46, 51–52.

INNER BEAUTY TIP

WHEN WE LOOK
THROUGH UNVEILED EYES,
WE WILL BEHOLD TRUTH,
FOR HE IS THE WAY, THE TRUTH
AND THE LIFE. THOSE WHO
NO LONGER FEAR TRUTH
WILL EMBRACE IT.

2

The Unveiling

Nevertheless when one turns to the Lord, the veil is taken away.
—2 Corinthians 3:16, NKJV

n order to unearth your inner beauty you will need to learn to remove the veil that hides it. Something is veiled in order to conceal, mask or cover it. Under many ancient and modern religions, women have veiled their faces and loosely draped their bodies with fabric to obscure their faces and hide their form in public. These are natural, outward masking techniques used to mute a woman's physical features and shape.

The Christian religion does not require that

women veil themselves outwardly. We are often proud that we are free from the bondage of physical veiling. Yet often we are unknowingly draped in a multitude of veils.

Veils can be used deliberately to hide us from the view of others. After forty days on the mountain with God, Moses used a veil to cover the reflected radiance of his face, which still shone brightly with the glory of God.

> But whenever he entered the LORD's presence to speak with him, he removed the veil until he came out. And when he came out and told the Israelites what he had been commanded, they saw that his face was radiant. Then Moses would put the veil back over his face until he went in to speak with the LORD.
>
> —EXODUS 34:34–35

We are told that Moses' face was radiant because he had spoken with the Lord (Exod. 34:29). The Israelites recognized this radiance as the product of being in God's presence. Moses let them see the light that shone from his face while he relayed the words of God; then he draped himself. He covered God's radiance until he again met with God. In His presence, Moses unveiled his face and spoke to God face to face as a man would speak to his friend. His face was veiled toward man and but naked before God.

Before the sacrifice of Jesus, each of us was separated from the presence of God by a veil. The holy of holies was hidden from the sight of all mankind except the high priest. A thick curtain separated the holy of holies from the holy place. It could only be entered by the high priest, and then only when he brought the blood for atonement.

With the death of Jesus, this heavy multilayered and colored veil was torn asunder.

> At that moment the curtain of the temple was torn in two from top to bottom. The earth shook and the rocks split.
> —MATTHEW 27:51

This was a supernatural demonstration. Due to its thickness, the veil would be difficult for man to tear from bottom to top, but impossible to tear from top to bottom. Even the rocks split in two the day Jesus died.

In the beginning God instructed His people to make altars upon rocks that had been neither carved nor chiseled. After the altars of stone came the tabernacle of Moses, then the temple. By splitting stones, God rent the old order from conception to completion. The old was finished and a new and living way had begun. From the first altar of stone all the way to the rending of the temple veil, the dispensation of Moses and the Law had yielded to the dispensation of the Spirit.

With the parting of the veil, the contents of the holy of holies were in clear view. Though it was unveiled, many Israelites still couldn't see.

The Rending of the Veil

Only in Christ is the veil that shrouds our hearts stripped away. (See 2 Corinthians 3:14–15.) The Law cannot remove the veil, for the Law itself had shrouded our hearts.

The reading of Moses is the reading of the Law. The Israelites wanted to see, but they were afraid to look. They wanted to listen, but they were afraid to hear. The children of Israel came to Moses and said to him, "You talk to God for us.

We don't want to talk to Him. Be our mediator; be our go-between. Tell us what He says to do, and we will do it."

> When the people saw the thunder and lightning and heard the trumpet and saw the mountain in smoke, they trembled with fear. They stayed at a distance and said to Moses, "Speak to us yourself and we will listen. But do not have God speak to us or we will die."
>
> —EXODUS 20:18–19

This separated the Israelites from direct contact with God. They had contact only with the man Moses, who had contact with God. Thus, the people were placed in a position to know *about* God without really knowing Him.

You can know all about someone, yet still not recognize that person if he or she walked right up to you. You have only heard about them and have never seen them; therefore, you do not recognize them face to face.

Conversely, you can visually know someone without knowing their voice. If you have never spoken with them, how could you recognize their voice if they were to call you on the phone? Only when you see them and hear them will you be able to match face and voice together.

Jesus came as *Immanuel,* or God with man. He was God incarnate. He could be seen, heard, spoken to and touched. In contrast, when God descended to the mountain to speak to the Israelites, they couldn't even touch the base of the mountain of God. Violation of such boundaries meant death.

Jesus was jostled, bumped and touched by a multitude of Israelites and some Gentiles. The fire of God did not break out and consume the people; instead, it reached out and healed them. Jesus is the union of God's Word, His holy fire and His boundless love.

The Law veils our hearts with the fear of judgment. The Israelites shook under the shadow and sound of God's law. They dared not approach Him and drew back while Moses drew near.

In contrast, the multitude pressed near to Jesus while the religious leaders drew back to plot His death. Though they had studied about Him, they did not recognize His voice or His face. They handled Him and questioned Him, but the veil remained over their hearts and blinded their eyes. This veil was more impenetrable than the temple's.

There is only one way to remove this veil created by the fear of judgment. It is through repentance. Paul explained the spiritual significance of this rent veil:

> Nevertheless when one turns to the Lord,
> the veil is taken away.
> —2 CORINTHIANS 3:16, NKJV

Turning to the Lord in repentance removes—rends—the veil from our hearts. It lifts the shroud that clouds our eyes so we can clearly see truth. Before this, all we saw was blurred and void of definite form and feature. But when the veil is swept away, there is clarity. There is freedom.

> Now the Lord is the Spirit; and where the Spirit of the Lord is, there is liberty. But we all, with unveiled face, beholding as in a mirror the glory of the Lord, are being transformed into the same image from glory to glory, just as by the Spirit of the Lord.
> —2 CORINTHIANS 3:17–18, NKJV

When our faces are unveiled we can see the true image in the mirror. If we veiled ourselves and approached our own reflections, even we could not accurately see ourselves. We could only perceive the hidden portion of our features by what had been unveiled. Others could never completely be certain if behind the veil there were smiles or frowns.

> Turning to the Lord in repentance removes—rends—the veil from our hearts.

Through Jesus this veil of distortion is snatched away. Our eyes then receive a portion of the revelation of God's glory. We can glimpse its radiance. As Moses, we bask in God's radiant presence. After we behold its beauty and truth, that same radiance is imparted to us, and we reflect what we have received. Thus begins the transformation process from our image to His, from glory to glory.

28

When we look through unveiled eyes, we will behold truth, for He is the way, the truth and the life. Those who no longer fear truth will embrace it. We will see it for what it is in the light of His mercy and grace.

Before turning to Christ, the truth did not set us free; it condemned us. We turned from its image because our own image varied so vastly from it. In fear of judgment, we ran and veiled ourselves with the Law or hid ourselves from God's view.

Our hearts condemned us, so we veiled our hearts, hoping to muffle and calm our fears. But our fears remained. Then we turned to Christ.

The same truth that once condemned us now brings life and liberty. Instead of judgment, we see freedom in the truth. The more we behold truth, the more we are transformed. This increases our capacity to radiate the light of God.

VEILED HEARTS

A veiled heart is not hidden from God. It only obscures our vision. This causes us to believe we're unseen.

I wear glasses or contacts to correct my vision.

Before I wore them, I was under the mistaken impression that no one saw me, because I could not see clearly. I would sing and bob my head in time to the music in my car, oblivious to the drivers on either side of me. If I didn't notice them, surely they didn't notice me. When I first got my glasses, I argued with the optometrist, "These are too strong! I can see everything!"

"You are supposed to," he countered.

"No, you don't understand," I insisted. "I can see leaves on the trees!"

With my former poor vision I saw a softer, blurred world. Trees were brown trunks with soft, shimmering green blobs on top. I was certain that once my vision was corrected, I would see these same images magnified, not clarified. With corrected eyesight, my world seemed smaller and less private. I noticed the people in cars, not just the cars. I wondered how often I had been waved to by people I knew, only to return their friendly greetings with blank stares.

My eyes had been veiled by nearsighted vision. When the veil was removed, I saw clearly, sometimes more clearly than I would have wished to see. I had enjoyed the soft-focus-lens look of my face. Now in the hard light of reality, I saw every freckle and pore. Looking in the mirror one day, I asked my husband, "Is this how you see me?"

"Is *what* how I see you?" he asked, looking perplexed.

"Can you see *this?*" I asked as I pointed to a brown spot on my face.

"Yes."

"Can you see *this?*" I asked, pointing to a blemish.

"Yes."

"Have you always seen these? I don't like the way I look when I can see," I murmured as I turned from the mirror and pulled off my glasses.

John came around behind me and turned me back toward the mirror. "Do you want me to tell you what I see?"

I really did, but in response, I just shrugged my shoulders.

"Put your glasses on and look in the mirror," John ordered.

While standing behind me, he pointed out to me what he saw each time he looked at me. He highlighted all the things he liked about my features. My focus shifted from the flaws to the love that overlooked them. I looked closer for the good John saw in me.

Our flaws have always been there, but God loves us in spite of them.

God does the same thing with us. When we first turn from our iniquities and behold our true images, we don't like what we see. We still see the remnants of the flaws, wrinkles and blemishes of our former lives. The clarification brings magnification to our shortcomings.

Just as I did with my glasses, I allowed the enemy to use my improved eyesight to point out my flaws. The flaws had always been there, and I had been loved in spite of them.

Our flaws have always been there, but God loves us in spite of them. He knows that correcting our blurred and darkened vision will cause us to accurately behold Him.

The enemy wants us to use this improved vision in a negative way to focus on ourselves. Then the Spirit encourages us to keep looking—*with unveiled face, beholding as in a mirror the glory of the Lord.* We don't look at ourselves with this unveiled vision; we look at the Lord.

Looking at our image does nothing to transform us—it simply discourages us. It limits us to ourselves. It is when we behold the glory of the Lord that we are *being transformed into the same image.*

To look deeper by the Spirit is to turn our focus from ourselves and toward Christ in us, the hope of glory. He speaks loving and comforting words to us as He patiently points us beyond the obvious, toward the glorious unseen.

IS IMAGE REALLY EVERYTHING?

The world says, "You are the surface; you are the image. *Image is everything!*" Well, image *is* everything to the world. The world looks in mirrors and beholds only its own veiled reflection. The world is limited to *self-image,* while we are being transformed into *God's image.*

33

Self-image is dependent on how you look, what you wear, what you have, with whom you hang out. It usually centers around beauty, youth, talent and money. All of these may vary or decrease with age.

God wants us to bask in His presence and then reflect His light to others.

Our image as Christians does not corrode or fade with the passing of our youth. It cannot be purchased with money. It cannot be won by talents and abilities. Our image comes from beholding our Father in the face of Jesus Christ and by washing ourselves in His Word.

God does not want us to veil our faces, as Moses did. He wants us to bask in His presence and then reflect His light to others.

> Therefore, since we have such a hope, we are very bold. We are not like Moses, who would put a veil over his face to keep the

Israelites from gazing at it while the radiance was fading away.

—2 Corinthians 3:12–13

Since we have a hope, we are *very bold*. Moses veiled the fading radiance of the Law. Though it was God-breathed and glorious, it was fleeting and temporary:

For if what is passing away was glorious, what remains is much more glorious.

—2 Corinthians 3:11, NKJV

Under the Law, the veil was all that could be seen, the shroud of separation between God and man. But our gospel is much more glorious. It is uncovered for our eyes to see, not shrouded in a thick cloud or separated by a thick curtain. It is there for all who turn to Christ.

Even if our gospel is veiled, it is veiled to those who are perishing. The god of this age has blinded the minds of unbelievers, so that they cannot see the light of the gospel of the glory of Christ, who is the image of God.

—2 Corinthians 4:3–4

What is the god of this age? I believe the answer has many facets, but the strongest explanation is self-worship, setting *ourselves* up as god. This happens when we are self-ruled, self-seeking, self-conscious, self-serving, self-motivated and *selfish*. It is evident when we are the center of our universe. Those without hope live behind veils—veils of guilt, veils of fear, veils of unbelief, veils of pride, veils of religion, veils of materialism and veils of rebellion. They shroud themselves in deception in order to hide from God.

> Nothing in all creation is hidden from God's sight. Everything is uncovered and laid bare before the eyes of him to whom we must give account.
>
> —HEBREWS 4:13

These veils ultimately fail to shield from the piercing and penetrating truth. Each of us will either be transformed by this light or judged by it. It is not safe to hide behind the veil; when we turn to the light, we're transformed.

It is comparable to stepping out from a cold, damp, dark cellar into the warmth and vibrancy of a sunlit backyard. The spring sun there caresses you with warmth. Sitting still, you can feel the sun's radiance penetrate your clothes and warm you to the bone. A chair invites you to sit down, and you bask in the gentle warmth of sunlight until every shudder and chill from the cold cellar is gone.

When you go indoors, you see reflected in your mirror the warm glow of the sun in the heightened flush of color on your skin. People look at you and know you have been in the sun. You don't have to tell them; they recognize the glow.

God wants us to *Son-bathe* so we can reflect His Son to others. If we *self-bathe*, no one will see His influence on us.

It is the same with Christians. We sit in the warmth of God's presence, basking in His truth, and come away glowing and recharged. God wants us to *Son-bathe* so we can reflect His Son to others. If we *self-bathe,* no one will see His influence on us.

BE TRANSFORMED

When we turned to Christ all of us were unveiled. But religion and the world often will attempt to shroud us again. Unknowingly, we can allow cultural influences to drape, disfigure and mask what God has done. These shrouds only hide our true image and worth. If we are being transformed to the image of Christ, then our worth is always increasing. Our beauty is maturing and softening. There is no reason to veil ourselves.

When we are first born again we see this radiance reflected in a gentleness and peace, which replaces our anxious fear of judgment and death. If we are not careful it is soon gone, and we are veiled once more. We lose the joy and boldness of our original rebirth and resign ourselves to settle for that fading reflection.

God is calling us to look at His reflection. If it is unclear and confused, then it has been shrouded in the graveclothes of religion and the works of the flesh. We need to stir ourselves to shake off the doubt that would cause us to shrink from His presence in fear of rejection.

The Lord wants to call us out of the cold, dark cellar and into the gentle warmth of the garden of the light of the knowledge of Him. Too often we are afraid to come into His presence, afraid the way will be barred by mistakes we have made since we became Christians. We are afraid our works are not good enough or numerous enough to grant us entrance. We are afraid that if we call, He will not answer. So we hide in fear of rejection, assuming it is better not to try than to be disappointed. We don't reach out, fearing we will be turned away.

In the dark cellar of doubt, we become pale and weak. Only mushrooms and mold grow in such damp darkness. Both feed on the remains of life. This darkness is the veil of the Law trying once again to separate us from God's light. The Law condemns and separates. The Spirit forgives and restores. We are admonished:

> Therefore, since we have a great high priest who has gone through the heavens, Jesus the Son of God, let us hold firmly to the faith we profess…Let us then approach the

39

throne of grace with confidence, so that we may receive mercy and find grace to help us in our time of need.

—Hebrews 4:14, 16

We have nothing to hide. We have boldness because of Christ. He is the perfect priest. He did not serve as a levitical priest, but as…

One who has become a priest not on the basis of a regulation as to his ancestry but on the basis of the power of an indestructible life. For it is declared: "You are a priest forever, in the order of Melchizedek." The former regulation is set aside because it was weak and useless (for the law made nothing perfect), and a better hope is introduced, by which we draw near to God.

—Hebrews 7:16–19

God wants you to be transformed even more than you want to be.

God wants us unveiled and confident as we come before Him in our time of need.

Do you know that God longs to speak to you more than you even want to hear from Him? He is waiting for you to turn to Him so He can remove any veils over your heart that may be separating you from glorious intimacy with Him! God wants you to be transformed even more than you want to be.

Adapted from *The True Measure of a Woman,* 85–97.

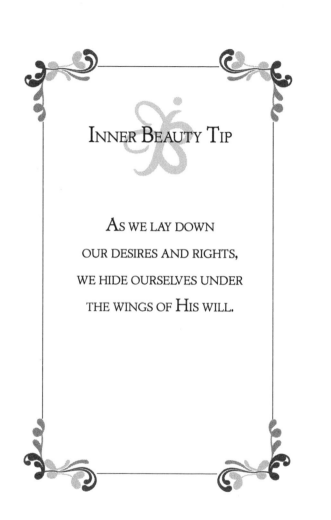

INNER BEAUTY TIP

As we lay down
our desires and rights,
we hide ourselves under
the wings of His will.

3

Desert
Daughters

Your beauty…should be that of your inner
self, the unfading beauty of a gentle and
quiet spirit.

—1 Peter 3:3–4

hen God refers to marriage, His reference is
not limited to or defined by our frail cultural perception.

"For your Maker is your husband—
    the Lord Almighty is his name—
the Holy One of Israel is your Redeemer;
    he is called the God of all the earth.
The Lord will call you back
    as if you were a wife deserted and dis-
        tressed in spirit—

43

a wife who married young,
only to be rejected," says your God.
"For a brief moment I abandoned you,
but with deep compassion I will bring
you back."

—Isaiah 54:5–7

Single or married, male or female, this promise stands as a covenant for every believer. God describes Himself as a Husband to an unfaithful wife whom He had put away in His anger, only to forgive, restore and draw her once more to Himself.

If you are a believer, you are part of the church and this is your marriage covenant.

He uses vivid and emotionally charged analogies to describe His relationship with His beloved Israel. But these analogies describe not only Israel the nation; they extend also to spiritual Israel—the children of promise.

DESERT DAUGHTERS

OUR MARRIAGE COVENANT

This relationship is described in the New Testament with this comparison:

> For this reason a man will leave his father
> and mother and be united to his wife, and
> the two will become one flesh. This is a
> profound mystery—but I am talking about
> Christ and the church.
>
> —EPHESIANS 5:31–32

If you are a believer, you are part of the church and this is your marriage covenant. Its principles, promises and provisions apply to you. They stand readily available for the single or married man or woman, Jew or Gentile. In Romans the strength of this new covenant is illustrated:

> Do you not know, brothers—for I am
> speaking to men who know the law—that
> the law has authority over a man only as
> long as he lives?
>
> For example, by law a married woman is
> bound to her husband as long as he is alive,
> but if her husband dies, she is released from
> the law of marriage. So then, if she marries

another man while her husband is still alive, she is called an adulteress.

But if her husband dies, she is released from that law and is not an adulteress, even though she marries another man.

So, my brothers, you also died to the law through the body of Christ, that you might belong to another, to him who was raised from the dead, in order that we might bear fruit to God.

—ROMANS 7:1–4

We belong to another. Our former husband was the law of sin and death; our new Husband is Christ. We have died to the old in order to be free to embrace the new. Notice this higher spiritual application is illustrated and explained by a lower natural one. The application of the natural to explain the spiritual does not negate the laws of the natural—it validates them. The deeper spiritual significance undergirds and upholds the laws of nature.

Therefore, the recognition of your Maker as your Husband does not negate the natural law of marriage. It supersedes and surrounds the lesser with the supernatural protection and provision of the greater. The recognition and application of this truth brings the revelation of marriage and its purpose. It is divinely rooted in companionship with God. A man, Adam, and his wife, Eve, exist in union as one with their Creator. This is God's divine plan.

> # If we allow Him to do so, the Holy Spirit will reveal God as our Husband.

From this point forward in this chapter, I am not addressing the natural issue of being single or married. I am speaking of the relationship between God and the believer.

If we allow Him to do so, the Holy Spirit will reveal God as our Husband. He is worthy of our trust, and His Word is worthy of our obedience. I pray you will study the scriptures in this chapter as though you were reading them for the first time.

Ageless Beauty

God used women to describe His bride and His church. Therefore, I believe God's instructions to women hold keys for all believers.

> Let not yours be the [merely] external adorning with [elaborate] interweaving and knotting of the hair, the wearing of jewelry, or changes of clothes; but let it be the inward adorning and beauty of the hidden person of the heart, with the incorruptible and unfading charm of a gentle and peaceful spirit, which [is not anxious or wrought up, but] is very precious in the sight of God.
>
> —1 Peter 3:3–4, amp

Notice it is precious to God when we trust Him. He sees the inner beauty others may miss. It never ages, fades or becomes corrupt. It is timeless and priceless. God treasures it. He guards and protects what is precious and valuable to Him.

> For it was thus that the pious women of old who hoped in God were [accustomed] to beautify themselves and were submissive to

48

their husbands [adapting themselves to
them as themselves secondary and dependent upon them].

—1 Peter 3:5, amp

We are beautified with fadeless, ageless beauty
when we submit and adapt our will to God's. As
we lay down our desires and rights, we hide ourselves under the wings of His will. Here is an application of God's ageless beauty:

It was thus that Sarah obeyed Abraham
[following his guidance and acknowledging
his headship over her by] calling him lord
(master, leader, authority).

—1 Peter 3:6, amp

When Sarah and Abraham traveled to foreign
nations, Abraham was afraid for his personal
safety because of Sarah's beauty. She was so beautiful that kings placed her in their harems, not
when she was young, but when she was in her sev-
enties or eighties. Abram told Sarai:

"Say you are my sister, so that I will be
treated well for your sake and my life will be
spared because of you." When Abram came

49

to Egypt, the Egyptians saw that she was a very beautiful woman. And when Pharaoh's officials saw her, they praised her to Pharaoh, and she was taken into his palace.
—Genesis 12:13–15

And Abimelech asked Abraham, "What was your reason for doing this?" Abraham replied, "I said to myself, 'There is surely no fear of God in this place, and they will kill me because of my wife.'"
—Genesis 20:10–11

God protected Sarah even when her husband placed his safety above hers. God moved in the supernatural realm to protect her from the kings who had taken her into their harems. God did this because she was a precious treasure to Him. We are to follow her example by acknowledging and submitting to God's guidance and His headship over us.

And you are now her true daughters if you do right and let nothing terrify you [not giving way to hysterical fears or letting anxieties unnerve you].
—1 Peter 3:6, amp

why are we the daughters of Sarah?

Sarah had no natural daughters. But this promise states we can be her true daughters. I believe we are the daughters of promise, the daughters of a free woman, when we behave like our mother, Sarah. This means we do what we know to be right, not yielding to our hysterical fears and not allowing worry to steal our courage.

> We are beautified with fadeless, ageless beauty when we submit and adapt our will to God's.

Sarah was a free woman. She was esteemed and honored because she esteemed and honored God and her husband. Hagar, on the other hand, was a slave woman, a captive who despised her mistress, Sarah. Hagar's offspring, Ishmael, followed his mother's pattern and mocked Isaac. Sarah understood there had to be a separation of the slave from the free.

Get rid of the slave woman and her son, for
the slave woman's son will never share in
the inheritance with the free woman's son.
—GALATIANS 4:30

Sarah's beauty was incorruptible, not only when she was young, but when she was old!

The slave woman's son was not the only one
denied a share of the inheritance. The slave
woman was cast out from her inheritance also.
Both the free woman and the slave woman had the
same husband. They both had sons. Yet their relationship with Abraham was very different. Hagar
represented the flesh and its bondage. Sarah represented spiritual freedom and the promise.
Galatians describes it this way:

His son by the slave woman was born in the
ordinary way; but his son by the free
woman was born as the result of a promise.

52

But why would you cast out a slave woman?

> These things may be taken figuratively, for the women represent two covenants. One covenant is from Mount Sinai and bears children who are to be slaves: This is Hagar. Now Hagar stands for Mount Sinai in Arabia and corresponds to the present city of Jerusalem, because she is in slavery with her children. But the Jerusalem that is above is free, and she is our mother.
>
> —GALATIANS 4:23–26

There it is again—the promise of descendants from Sarah. Sarah's beauty was incorruptible, not only when she was young, but when she was old! She was a natural foreshadowing of the ageless, fadeless beauty found in Christ.

SARAH'S BEAUTY REGIMEN

It is obvious from these accounts that Sarah was a woman of exceptional beauty. So let's take a closer look at her beauty regimen.

1. She left all that was comfortable and familiar.
2. She followed her husband to a strange land.

3. She lived in a tent in the desert.
4. She trusted God and did not fear or worry.

This was not the life of a pampered queen in a palace. It was a life of constant transition and faith. She would settle (if you call living in a tent "settling") in one place for a while, then travel across the desert to another. She was always waiting for the fulfillment of God's promise and trusting the guidance of her husband. She honored and obeyed her husband, and he honored and obeyed God.

There is no record that she complained. She never looked back at what she left behind. Abraham, the father of faith, and his princess, Sarah, are an example and pattern of Christ and His bride, the church.

We are called to adapt ourselves as dependent and secondary to Christ.

Christ is our Head, and all who believe are subject to His lordship, leadership and authority. We are called to adapt ourselves as dependent and secondary to Christ. But we have no reason to fear. He is our Maker-Husband. He has forged us with His love.

Adapted from Lisa Bevere, *Out of Control and Loving It!*, 81–87.

Inner Beauty Tip

God is wooing a bride
from among His church,
one who loves Him
because she cannot
live without Him.

4

Is Jesus Coming for a Wife or a Bride?

He has clothed me with garments of salvation and arrayed me in a robe of righteousness...as a bride adorns herself with her jewels.

—Isaiah 61:10

hen a man marries a bride she becomes his wife, right? Yes, this is true. But is it possible to be a wife and not be a bride? Most of us know the definition of a wife, but what about a bride? We were brides for such a short time we have forgotten what it was like altogether.

COMPANIONSHIP

When John and I were engaged, I was his bride. We were head over heels in love with each other for no

57

reason other than we felt made for each other. We were certain God had brought us together. We counted the days and hours that separated us and anxiously anticipated our time together. When we were with each other nothing else seemed to matter. All other pressures or distractions seemed to fall away.

John did not ask me to marry him because I was a good cook, a great mother, a good housekeeper, a wonderful helpmate or financially responsible. I had not proved I could be any of these things. He had not required I prove my aptitude in any area. He knew he had my heart, and that was enough for him.

He proposed because he loved me and felt incomplete without me. It did not seem to matter whether I would ever bear a child, keep a house, balance a checkbook or stand beside him in ministry. He married me for one reason—companionship.

God brought Eve out of Adam's side for this same reason. Adam was lonely for someone who was like himself. God put Adam into a deep sleep and removed a rib from his side, which God used to create Eve. Then God presented her to Adam (Gen. 2:21–23). Eve had been hidden in Adam all along. They came together again as one but in a new and different way—separate and yet one.

God's grace is truly amazing, for His mercy triumphs over our judgment.

In the same way, the Father has prepared us as the bride of Christ. The death of Christ, the second Adam, brought forth His bride, the church. Christ's side was pierced, and the blood and water flowed as He entered into the sleep of death. Now we, as the bride, anxiously await the marriage supper of the Lamb where we will see Him face to face and be joined together with Him forever.

God's grace is truly amazing, for His mercy triumphs over our judgment. Though we deserved death, He redeemed us to be His only Son's bride and companion forever. This positions us as His children.

He did not redeem us to enslave us. It is for freedom that Christ has set us free (Gal. 5:1). He does not want us to work *for* Him. He redeemed us so that we may work *alongside* Him. We can do nothing of eternal value apart from Him, so it is foolish to think we can do anything *for* Him. We only produce what is acceptable and life giving when we work *with* Him, through His strength, His life and His Spirit.

ACCEPTABLE OFFERING

Abel's sacrifice was accepted because he followed the pattern God had established in the garden. An innocent animal was to be slain and offered to cover the nakedness and transgressions of man.

Abel was a keeper of sheep. God supplied the grass, grain and water that nourished Abel's flocks. Abel only tended them. At the appointed time Abel separated the firstborn lamb from his flock to give to the Lord.

His brother Cain labored as a tiller of the ground. He planted, cultivated, tended and harvested his crops, but when God rejected the offering from his crops, he was enraged and became jealous of his brother.

> Then the LORD said to Cain, "Why are you
> angry? Why is your face downcast? If you
> do what is right, will you not be accepted?
> But if you do not do what is right, sin is
> crouching at your door; it desires to have
> you, but you must master it."
>
> —GENESIS 4:6–7

God did not reject Cain—He rejected his offering. Cain was not able to make that distinction. He felt rejected and isolated. God noticed this, and He encouraged him to do right and overcome this sin that crouched at his door. Cain had the same opportunity as Abel to present an acceptable sacrifice, but Cain did not listen to God's advice.

More than likely Adam had instructed his sons that animal sacrifice was the acceptable method of preparing an offering for God. Otherwise, how would Abel have known what to do? Perhaps animal sacrifice seemed too simple to Cain. Maybe he wanted to present something he had produced to God. Whatever the reason, it appeared Cain was too busy laboring *for* God to labor *with* Him.

It is easier to attack those around us than to admit we have done things in our own way and by our own strength. So Cain rose up and killed the brother he believed God favored.

> Now Cain said to his brother Abel, "Let's go out to the field." And while they were in the field, Cain attacked his brother Abel and killed him.
>
> —GENESIS 4:8

HIS LABOR OR OURS?

When we work *for* God instead of *with* God, we lose sight of God's character, nature and perspective. Our motives become distorted and mixed. We become religious (serve God our way instead of His), legalistic (by the parameters and restrictions of man), judgmental (critical of all outside our understanding) and proud of our own accomplishments ("look how hard I have worked"). Soon we are presenting the works of our hands and the labor of our flesh to God for His blessing. But He will not bless that.

Frustrated, we begin to strive with our brothers. Envy stirs our hearts against those who are laboring acceptably. We are tempted to believe we deserve more because we are working harder. *Why should they be blessed?* The enemy wants to deceive us into believing they have removed or displaced the favor we feel is due us.

When we work *for* God instead of *with* God, we lose sight of God's character, nature and perspective.

God's favor and acceptance are available to everyone, but they are given on *His* terms, not ours. God imparts a righteousness born of the spirit and contrary to our natural reason (Gal. 5:5). It cannot be earned by works; therefore it cannot be kept by them. It is a gift. We receive it based on Jesus' righteousness and God's love.

Religion is restrictive and self-righteous. It labors to produce while the Spirit produces without labor. Unfortunately, many in the church are busy being "religious wives" while God is waiting and watching for a loving bride.

I believe God is wooing a bride from among His church—one who loves Him because she cannot live without Him.

BRIDE VS. WIFE

To explain the concept of being a bride, let's look at the story of Hannah. Hannah was one of the two wives of Elkanah. She is mentioned first, which indicates he married her first. It was probably due to Hannah's barrenness that Elkanah chose to marry a second wife, Peninnah. Elkanah's second wife bore him many children, while Hannah's barrenness continued for years. Hannah was loved and cared for by her husband, yet there was a hunger stirring in her for more. This was evident when the family went to worship before the Lord.

> Whenever the day came for Elkanah to sacrifice, he would give portions of the meat to his wife Peninnah and to all her sons and daughters. But to Hannah he gave a double portion because he loved her, and the LORD had closed her womb. And because the LORD

64

had closed her womb, her rival kept provoking her in order to irritate her. This went on year after year. Whenever Hannah went up to the house of the LORD, her rival provoked her till she wept and would not eat.

—1 Samuel 1:4–7

Even though Hannah was honored by her husband with a double portion, she could not enjoy it because she was so tormented by her adversary. How could God allow this? Notice it was God, not the devil, who closed Hannah's womb. Why? I believe God closed it to create a divine hunger in Hannah, one greater than a child could satisfy, one only He could fulfill.

> I believe God is wooing a bride from among His church—one who loves Him because she cannot live without Him.

65

Hannah loved her husband, but she had learned through the adversity she experienced that he was not her source of life. God was. She watched as Peninnah bore her husband's sons. Elkanah's name was established, yet still she hungered for more. No matter how wonderful her husband was to her, it was not enough to fill the gnawing void in her heart.

Brokenness and humility were woven into Hannah's nature. All the longing, disappointment and torment created a womb that could bear a prophetic seed.

I believe Hannah was a bride. Because God was her source of life, she was a giver, not a taker. This is why her husband loved Hannah more than Peninnah, even though it appeared she produced less.

Year after year she prayed for a son. At first her motive might have been, "God, give me a son for my husband's name sake." Then it may have changed to, "God, give me a son because of my adversary." But when it became, "God, give me son, and I will give him to You," God gave to her the desire of her heart.

Hannah made a vow, saying:

> O LORD Almighty, if you will only look
> upon your servant's misery and remember
> me, and not forget your servant but give
> her a son, then I will give him to the Lord
> for all the days of his life, and no razor will
> ever be used on his head.
>
> —1 SAMUEL 1:11

Hannah had called the life of God into an empty, barren womb. Not just the natural life of a child, but of one set apart and inspired by God. Out of her despair she consecrated and conceived the child Samuel. He was the prophetic voice of God to a lost and straying Israel.

Both women were married to the same husband but with very different relationships. Peninnah was the religious wife, while Hannah was the love-struck bride. Following are some contrasts between these two women:

- Hannah was barren and loved, while Peninnah was fruitful and used.

- Hannah was broken and sought God, not just religious activities.

Peninnah was proud of her offspring and comfortable with the religious. She despised Hannah because Elkanah loved Hannah even though she produced no children.

- Hannah denied herself the joy of raising her child in order to give him to the Lord. Peninnah appeared to be concerned only with herself and cared nothing for the feelings of others.

- Hannah was her husband's love while Peninnah was his wife.

After Samuel, Hannah bore five more children while Peninnah had no more (1 Sam. 2:21). She had already fulfilled her purpose.

It would appear Hannah's nature and motives were very different from Peninnah's. We glimpse Peninnah's nature in her prophetic prayer on the advent of Samuel's dedication:

> Do not keep talking so proudly or let your mouth speak such arrogance, for the LORD is a God who knows, and by him deeds are

> weighed... Those who were full hire themselves out for food, but those who were hungry hunger no more. She who was barren has borne seven children, but she who has had many sons pines away.
>
> —1 Samuel 2:3, 5

Peninnah had comforted herself with the children she had produced. She had been full while Hannah had hungered. Now Peninnah watched as her children were displaced by the children of Hannah, the favored wife.

I believe these two wives prophetically represent the condition of the church. There are barren brides crying out for more, and there are satisfied wives who remain silent. The brides love and are loved by God. They are intimate with Him. They have been broken and humbled by their adversaries. The persecution wrought the godly character of meekness into their nature. They will not touch the glory, but return it all back to God. They have not forgotten why they love—they are His bride.

How's Your Appetite?

What I have seen God do in the past and what I see

Him doing right now are both wonderful. But I am hungry for something I have yet to see, taste or handle. I rejoice for what the body of Christ has experienced, but I hunger for more.

This desire for more began to stir in my heart until I felt I was pregnant with it. Then God challenged me: "If you want more than what you've seen, you'll need to be more than you've been. You'll need to give more than you've given." At each new level in our walks with God there is an increase of commitment and separation.

One morning as I prayed for my family, I asked God to increase my children's hunger for Him. Deep in my spirit I heard His response, "If your children are not hungry, it is because they are already full."

Just as natural hunger comes when we are empty and leaves when we are full, so it is with the hunger of the Spirit. Therefore, I will only be hungry when I am not already full. To develop this spiritual hunger I will need to fast all that is not of God that tries to fill me. To explain, let's look again at Hannah.

Hannah fasted her double portion of food and

favor, and prostrated herself before God. She refused to be comforted merely by the favor of man. She wanted the favor of God. In her day barrenness was a reproach. When her husband gave her a double portion of meat at the religious feast, it said to those present, "I love this woman. Though she has not borne me a child, she has my favor." But Hannah had come to the place where this double portion of her husband's love and favor was not enough. So she cried out to God, aware that only His provision could satisfy her.

In the midst of religious activities and worldly distractions it is important that we deny ourselves their fleeting satisfactions and cry out for more. Like Hannah, we need to cry out to the Most High until He answers our deepest yearnings. We are to deny our souls the satisfaction of the temporal and cry out for the eternal.

> A satisfied soul loathes the honeycomb, but
> to a hungry soul every bitter thing is sweet.
> —Proverbs 27:7, nkjv

This example is not merely limited to food. To those who hunger for God, even His correction is refreshing. That is why the barren woman can sing.

> "Sing, O barren woman, you who never
> bore a child; burst into song, shout for joy,
> you who were never in labor; because more
> are the children of the desolate woman
> than of her who has a husband," says the
> Lord.
>
> —Isaiah 54:1

God is calling us back to our first love. There we will find the strength and sustenance to remain a bride.

We are to deny our souls the satisfaction of the temporal and cry out for the eternal.

John and I have four children. All were born out of intimacy. We were not intimate in order to have children. We have children because we have been intimate. Likewise, God wants our spiritual offspring to be the product of intimacy with Him.

We are not to pursue Jesus in order to get salvation, finances, ministry, anointing, healing or anything else. All these are found when we lose ourselves in Him.

About five years ago while I prepared to minister at a women's meeting, I prayed my same old, pious prayer: "God, just use me to minister to these women..." God interrupted me with a question.

"Lisa, have you ever been used by a friend?"

"Yes," I answered hesitantly.

"How did you like it?"

"I didn't. I felt betrayed."

"Have you ever been used by a boyfriend?"

"Yes," I answered.

"How did you like it?"

"I didn't. I felt cheap and dirty."

Then God replied, "I don't use people. Satan does. I heal them, anoint them, transform and conform them to My image, but I do not use them."

I was shocked. I had always been taught to pray that way, but suddenly I could see how absurd it was to think of God as a user and a taker.

God told me that it grieves Him when ministers allow Him only limited access into a few areas of their ministry while barring His access to other areas. The area most frequently denied is His influence in our personal lifestyles.

The areas we hold back from God eventually become our downfall. I don't know how many times I have heard someone say, "I just don't understand how someone who was so anointed to preach could become an alcoholic or abuse his or her family or commit adultery. God had used him or her so mightily. How could this happen?"

It is always God's desire to flow through every area of our being, not just in the area of ministry. We are the ones who limit God. It is my prayer that His anointing will spill into every area of my life, that not one area will remain untouched by His presence.

KNOWN BY GOD

We know that we all possess knowledge. Knowledge puffs up, but love builds up. The man who thinks he knows something does not yet know as he ought to know. But the man who loves God is known by God.

—1 CORINTHIANS 8:1–3

It is not the amount of knowledge we have that produces life. Life is found in the knowledge that we live. Is it better to have knowledge of God or to be known by Him? You can know about someone but still not have a relationship with that person. It is of utmost importance that we are known by God.

It is not the amount of
knowledge we have
that produces life.
Life is found in the
knowledge that we live.

When Jesus spoke in the Gospels about entrance to the kingdom of heaven being denied to someone, it was followed by this explanation: "Depart, I do not know you." They knew Him, but He did not know them. How tragic to know about someone without ever taking the time to let that person know you.

The psalmist cried, "Search me, O God, and know my heart" (Ps. 139:23). He wanted God to delve into the deepest recesses of his soul until he was known by God. It is in this process that we are transformed by the light of His Word. It is through this process that we develop a heart that can love God. We are transformed from wives to brides. May you hunger to know even as you are known so that you might love even as you are loved.

Adapted from *Out of Control and Loving It!*, 49–60.

Conclusion

ow that we've established how the daughter of Zion is set free, the question is, When will she loose herself of her chains? How will she let her inner beauty be unveiled to radiate forth to all around her?

Your inner beauty will only be unveiled when you throw off the veil yourself:

> But when you grow restless, you will throw
> his yoke from off your neck.
> —Genesis 27:40

Notice it did not say, "When God thinks you can't take it anymore He will take the yoke off you." Nor did it say, "When God decides you have suffered enough He will remove the yoke." In fact, God is not even mentioned in this verse, but we find the words *you* or *your* are mentioned three times.

Paraphrased, it could read, "When you've had enough, you will throw off your veil. When you've stopped blaming everyone else; when you stop feeling sorry for yourself; when you stop searching for a person or organization to help you; when you no longer look back; when you stop blaming God; when you are finally frustrated with the limitations of your yoke; when you are tired enough to get mad; then you'll break free."

Go Ahead, Get Mad

After John and I were married for one year, he quit a secure engineering position with good pay to take a service position at our local church. His earnings were almost half of what they had been previously. At that point I waved good-bye to the idea of ever owning a house.

As a couple we had agreed to lay aside our financial security and pursue in earnest the call of God on our lives. No sooner than we set our hearts to do so, our finances came under attack from every direction. One morning I went out to my car and found the window shattered in pieces on the car seat. There was no apparent reason for the break, so we had to blame it on the relentless Texas heat. The car was not fit to drive, and we did not have the money to fix it.

I took a job to help out, but the onslaught seemed to drain everything. No longer was I dreaming wistfully of a house. I was worried if I would have enough to buy gas and food until the next paycheck came.

> ## "When you've had enough you will throw off your veil."

John and I tithed faithfully and gave offerings, yet it seemed we were robbed on every side. One night we attended a service where people were testifying about God's faithfulness in blessing their finances. I thought to myself, *I don't care about blessing. At this point I would just like provision.* After the service we both were so discouraged that we sat in John's car and cried. We promised each other not even to hint about our financial need to anyone. If God did not take care of us, we would do without.

The next day while home for lunch, I read all the scriptures I could find about finances and provision. Frustrated, I stomped my foot and said aloud, "God, You said You'd meet my needs. Well, You're not!"

He answered back, "I am not standing between you and your finances."

I was bewildered. I knew we were doing everything on our end to keep the covenant we had made with God. We had confessed, believed, given offerings and tithed. The only thing we had not done was receive. God had told me He was not withholding the finances from us. So who was?

Then I got mad. Right there in my kitchen I yelled, "It is written that God will meet my needs according to His riches in glory. These are needs. Devil, I command you to get your hands off our finances. We will not back down from the call of God upon our lives. Let God be true no matter what it looks like."

I actually felt something happen within me. I was excited and hopeful even though I had not done anything except stand in my kitchen and shout. I called John at the office and said, "Honey, something has happened. God is not the problem. The devil is!" John was so excited. God had shown him the same thing on his lunch hour. We both rejoiced. We were rich in faith.

God is not holding out on you! He is cheering you on!

That night after service, a couple who had visited the church pulled us aside. They shared that God had told them to give us some money. Then they handed us an envelope and left. When we got home we were shocked to discover it contained what we needed to fix my car with enough left over to buy groceries and gas.

Some of you need to yell in your kitchen! You have put up with harassment and captivity so long it has become a way of life. Don't let timidity and past failures hold you down. God is not holding out on you! He is cheering you on!

When my boys first started to walk, they enjoyed venturing the short distance from sofa to table. They would walk farther if we all cheered and clapped. They would stand and screech to get everyone's attention, take a few steps and clap for themselves.

But the day came when they realized that walking was not just for show; it was for keeps. Suddenly they did not think it was so much fun. They had to work hard to keep up the pace. They would plop down on their diapered bottoms and wail for someone to pick them up so they could ride on a hip.

Often I would move out of reach and encourage them, "Come on, you can do it!" They knew they could, but it was easier not to. They wanted to be carried.

Now I can't slow them down. Walking is no longer a problem. They are running everywhere! They even do things on Rollerblades that scare me! They discovered the joy of independent mobility. When they got tired of sitting and waiting to be picked up, they stood, walked and then ran.

Don't sit on the floor waiting for someone to

pick you up. If you are restless, God is calling you not only to walk but to run—free and untethered. You don't have to wait for the next seminar to cut loose. You don't have to figure it all out first. Just get mad and get free!

Allow the faith of God to open your eyes to see what doubt and discouragement have hidden from your view. When you do—and you begin to run in the blessings God has for the woman of God—then your inner beauty will shine forth. The veil will have been cast away forever, and you will radiate the glory of your heavenly Husband, Christ Himself.

Adapted from *Out of Control and Loving It!*, pages 41–42, 44–47.

If you are enjoying the Inner Beauty Series by Lisa Bevere, here are some other titles from Charisma House that we think will minister to you...

Out of Control and Loving It!
Lisa Bevere
ISBN: 0-88419-436-1
Retail Price: $12.99

Lisa Bevere's life was a whirlwind of turmoil until she discovered that whenever she was in charge, things ended up in a mess. *Out of Control and Loving It!* is her journey from fearful, frantic control to a haven of rest and peace under God's control.

You Are Not What You Weigh
Lisa Bevere
ISBN: 0-88419-661-5
Retail Price: $10.99

Are you tired of reading trendy diet books, taking faddish pills and ordering the latest in infomercial exercise equipment? This is not another "how-to-lose-weight" book. Dare to believe, and this will be the last book you'll need to finally end your war with food and break free from the bondage of weight watching.

The True Measure of a Woman
Lisa Bevere
ISBN: 0-88419-487-6
Retail Price: $11.99

In her frank, yet gentle manner, Lisa Bevere exposes the subtle influences and blatant lies that hold many women captive. With the unveiling truth of God's Word, she displaces these lies and helps you discover who you are in Christ.

 To pick up a copy of any of these titles, contact your local Christian bookstore or order online at www.charismawarehouse.com.